THE
PSALMS
AROUND
US

THE PSALMS AROUND US

COUNTRYSIDE PRESS
Farm Journal, Inc., Philadelphia, Pa.

DOUBLEDAY & COMPANY, INC.
GARDEN CITY, NEW YORK

Quotations from the Psalms are from the
Revised Standard version of the Bible, used by permission

Published by Countryside Press, a division of Farm Journal, Inc.,
Washington Square, Philadelphia, Pennsylvania

Copyright ©, by Farm Journal, Inc., 1970
All rights reserved

Library of Congress catalog card number 72-114340

Photographs in this book are by Grant Heilman, except
those on pages 9 and 10, courtesy of NASA

Book design: Al J. Reagan

Distributed to the book trade by Doubleday & Company, Inc.,
Garden City, New York

CONTENTS

On earth
as in heaven

Three thousand years ago in a different language in a far country, another human being asked, like the astronaut, *What is man that thou art mindful of him?* In his kinship with the universe, David marveled *Thou hast made man little less than God.* He looked around him at the rich beauty, the glory, the power of the *earth given to the sons of men* and put his feelings into words—psalms.

The dialogue between the inner better self of Everyman and his God is eternal. His pride at walking on the moon is tempered with a new sense of divinity.

We scan with new wonder the familiar vistas; we see a hill, a tree, a bud in sharper relief. Shaken by a new view of heaven, we need the reassurance of the earth.

Beautiful scenes . . . the bounty and artistry of the universe . . . inspire our best thoughts and, subsequently, deeds. As steel towers rise to compete with the glacier-carved hills, as swaths of concrete crowd back the fresh, yielding earth, nature's beauty becomes more precious.

We have collected in this book scenes from our country and our time. The words which they illustrate anew will forever be timeless.

THE HEAVENS
TELL THE GLORY
OF GOD

When I look at thy heavens, the
    work of thy fingers,
the moon and the stars which
    thou hast established;
what is man that thou art mindful
    of him,
    and the son of man that thou
    dost care for him?   8:3,4

Yet thou hast made him little less
　　than God,
and dost crown him with glory
　　and honor.　8:5

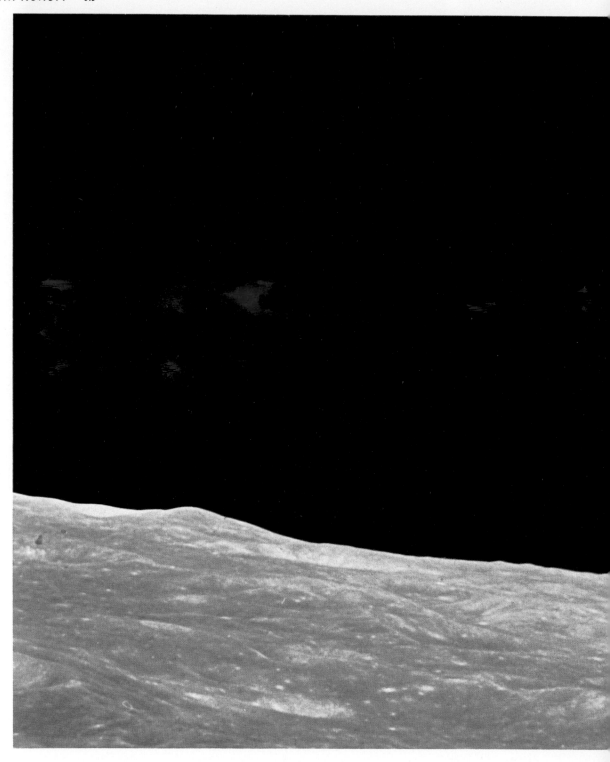

O give thanks to the Lord,
    for he is good,
    for his steadfast love endures for
      ever.
To him who made the great lights,
    for his steadfast love endures for
      ever;
the sun to rule over the day,
    for his steadfast love endures for
      ever;
the moon and stars to rule over
      the night,
    for his steadfast love endures for
    ever   136:1,7-9

The heavens are telling the
    glory of God;
  and the firmament proclaims his
    handiwork.
In them he has set a tent for the
    sun,
which comes forth like a bride-
    groom leaving his chamber,
  and like a strong man runs its
    course with joy.
Its rising is from the end of the
    heavens,
  and its circuit to the end of them;
  and there is nothing hid from its
    heat.   *19:1,4-6*

*For I know that the Lord is great,
and that our Lord is above all
gods.
Whatever the Lord pleases he
does,
in heaven and on earth,
in the seas and all deeps.
He it is who makes the clouds rise
at the end of the earth,
who makes lightnings for the
rain
and brings forth the wind from
his storehouses.* 135:5-7

*The clouds poured out water;
the skies gave forth thunder;
thy arrows flashed on every side.
The crash of thy thunder was in
the whirlwind;
thy lightnings lighted up the
world;
the earth trembled and shook.* 77:17,18

$\mathbb{T}$he heavens proclaim his righteousness;
and all the peoples behold his glory.   97:6

THE EARTH
IS THE LORD'S
AND
THE FULNESS THEREOF

The earth is the Lord's and
    the fulness thereof,
  the world and those who dwell
    therein;
for he has founded it upon the seas,
  and established it upon the rivers.
Who shall ascend the hill of the
    Lord?
  And who shall stand in his holy
    place?
He who has clean hands and a pure
    heart,

who does not lift up his soul to
    what is false,
  and does not swear deceitfully.
He will receive blessing from the
    Lord,
  and vindication from the God of
    his salvation.
Such is the generation of those who
    seek him,
  who seek the face of the God of
    Jacob.   24:1-6

He divided the sea and let them
    pass through it,
    and made the waters stand like
      a heap.
In the daytime he led them with a
    cloud,
    and all the night with a fiery
      light.
He cleft rocks in the wilderness,
    and gave them drink abundantly
      as from the deep.
He made streams come out of the
    rock,
    and caused waters to flow down
      like rivers.   78:13-16

Who turns the rock into a pool of
    water,
the flint into a spring of water.   114:8

Thou visitest the earth and
    waterest it,
  thou greatly enrichest it;
the river of God is full of water;
  thou providest their grain,
  for so thou hast prepared it.
Thou waterest its furrows
    abundantly,
  settling its ridges,
softening it with showers,
  and blessing its growth.   65:9,10

The pastures of the wilderness drip,
the hills gird themselves with joy,
the meadows clothe themselves
with flocks,

the valleys deck themselves with
grain,
they shout and sing together for
joy.   65:12,13

He gives snow like wool;
he scatters hoarfrost like ashes.
He casts forth his ice like morsels;
who can stand before his cold?

He sends forth his word, and melts
them;
he makes his wind blow, and the
waters flow. 147:18

BUT THE EARTH
HE HAS GIVEN
TO THE SONS OF MEN

Thou hast given him dominion over
 the works of thy hands;
 thou hast put all things under his
 feet,
all sheep and oxen,
 and also the beasts of the field   8:6,7

The birds of the air, and the fish of
    the sea,
whatever passes along the paths
    of the sea.   8:8

O Lord, our Lord,
how majestic is thy name in all
    the earth!   8:9

He covers the heavens with clouds,
he prepares rain for the earth,
he makes grass grow upon the
    hills.
He gives to the beasts their food,
    and to the young ravens which
    cry.   147:8,9

36

He makes peace in your borders; he fills you with the finest of the wheat. 147:14

They sow fields, and <u>plant vineyards,</u>
　　and get a fruitful yield.
By his blessing they multiply
　　　greatly;
　　and he does not let their cattle
　　　decrease.　　107 · ²⁷ 38

The earth has yielded its increase;
　　<u>God, our God, has blessed us.</u>
God has blessed us;
　　let all the ends of the earth fear
　　　him!　　67:6,7

The plowers plowed upon my back;
they made long their furrows.   129:3

I will sing to the Lord,
   because he has dealt bountifully
      with me.   13:6

May the Lord give you increase,
   you and your children!
May you be blessed by the Lord,
   who made heaven and earth!
The heavens are the Lord's
      heavens,
   but the earth he has given to the
      sons of men.   115:14-16

THE LORD
IS MY SHEPHERD

*The Lord is my shepherd, I
shall not want;
he makes me lie down in green
pastures.* 23:1,2

He leads me beside still waters   23:2

He restores my soul.
He leads me in paths of righteousness
for his name's sake.   23:3

Even though I walk through the
  valley of the shadow
 I fear no evil;
for thou art with me;
 thy rod and thy staff,
 they comfort me. 23:4

Thou preparest a table before me
in the presence of my enemies;
thou anointest my head with oil,
my cup overflows.   23:5

Surely goodness and mercy shall
follow me
all the days of my life;
and I shall dwell in the house of
the Lord
for ever. 23:6

GREAT IS HIS
STEADFAST LOVE

Blessed is the man
    who walks not in the counsel of
        the wicked,
nor stands in the way of sinners,
    nor sits in the seat of scoffers;
but his delight is in the law of the
        Lord,
    and on his law he meditates day
        and night.

He is like a tree
    planted by streams of water,
that yields its fruit in its season,
    and its leaf does not wither.
In all that he does, he prospers.   1:1-3

57

As for man, his days are like grass;
  he flourishes like a flower of the
    field;
for the wind passes over it, and it
    is gone,
  and its place knows it no more.
But the steadfast love of the Lord
    is from everlasting to
    everlasting
  upon those who fear him,
  and his righteousness to
    children's children,
to those who keep his covenant
  and remember to do his
    commandments. *103:15-18*

In thee, O Lord, do I seek
    refuge;
    let me never be put to shame;
    in thy righteousness deliver me!
Incline thy ear to me,
    rescue me speedily!
Be thou a rock of refuge for me,
    a strong fortress to save me!
Yea, thou art my rock and my
    fortress;
    for thy name's sake lead me and
    guide me   *31:1-3*

Thy steadfast love, O Lord,
    extends to the heavens,
    thy faithfulness to the clouds.
Thy righteousness is like the moun-
    tains of God,
    thy judgments are like the great
    deep;
man and beast thou savest,
    O Lord.   36:5,6

Know that the Lord is God!
It is he that made us, and we are
his;
we are his people, and the sheep
of his pasture.   100:3

Then we thy people, the flock of
thy pasture,
will give thanks to thee for ever;
from generation to generation we
will recount thy praise.   79:13

The Lord looks down from heaven,
   he sees all the sons of men;
from where he sits enthroned he
     looks forth
   on all the inhabitants of the
     earth,
he who fashions the hearts of them
    all,
   and observes all their deeds.   33:13-15

Behold, how good and
   pleasant it is
when brothers dwell in unity!   133:1

MANIFOLD
ARE
THY WORKS

Bless the Lord, O my soul!
  O Lord my God, thou art
    very great!

Thou art clothed with honor and
    majesty,
  who coverest thyself with light as
    with a garment,
who hast stretched out the heavens
    like a tent. . .

who makest the clouds thy chariot,
  who ridest on the wings of the
    wind,
who makest the winds thy
    messengers,
  fire and flame thy ministers.
Thou didst set the earth on its
    foundations,
  so that it should never be shaken.   104:1-5

The mountains rose, the valleys
    sank down
  to the place which thou didst
    appoint for them.
Thou didst set a bound which they
    should not pass,
  so that they might not again
    cover the earth.
Thou makest springs gush forth in
    the valleys. . .
they give drink to every beast of the
    field;
  the wild asses quench their thirst.
By them the birds of the air have
    their habitation;
  they sing among the branches.   *104:8-12*

Thou dost cause the grass to grow
  for the cattle,
    and plants for man to cultivate,
  that he may bring forth food from
    the earth. . .
  The trees of the Lord are watered
    abundantly. . .
  In them the birds build their nests;
    the stork has her home in the fir
    trees.
  The high mountains are for the
    wild goats;
    the rocks are a refuge for the
    badgers.   104:14-18

72

Thou hast made the moon to mark
    the seasons;
  the sun knows its time for setting
Thou makest darkness, and it is
    night   104:19,20

When the sun rises...
Man goes forth to his work
and to his labor until the evening.   104:22,23

O Lord, how manifold are thy
    works! . . .
Yonder is the sea, great and wide,
   which teems with things
      innumerable,
   living things both small and
      great.   104:24,25

These all look to thee,
to give them their food in due
season.
When thou givest to them, they
gather it up;
when thou openest thy hand,
they are filled with good
things.
I will sing to the Lord as long as
I live;
I will sing praise to my God
while I have being.
May my meditation be pleasing to
him,
for I rejoice in the Lord. . .
Bless the Lord, O my soul!
Praise the Lord! 104:27,28,33-35

I LIFT UP
MY EYES

Be still, and know that I am God.
I am exalted among the nations,
I am exalted in the earth!"
The Lord of hosts is with us;
the God of Jacob is our
refuge. 46:10,11

I lift up my eyes to the
  hills.
From whence does my help
  come?
My help comes from the Lord,
  who made heaven and earth.   121:1,2

Hear my cry, O God,
    listen to my prayer;
from the end of the earth I call to
        thee,
    when my heart is faint.
Lead thou me
    to the rock that is higher than I;
for thou art my refuge,
    a strong tower against the enemy.   61:1-3

He made the storm be still,
  and the waves of the sea were
    hushed.
Then they were glad because they
    had quiet,
  and he brought them to their
    desired haven.

Let them thank the Lord for his
    steadfast love,
  for his wonderful works to the
    sons of men!
Let them extol him in the congre-
    gation of the people,
  and praise him in the assembly
    of the elders.   107:29-32

*W*hen peoples gather together,
and kingdoms, to worship the
Lord.   102:22

*L*et us go to his dwelling place;
let us worship at his footstool!''   132:7

I was glad when they said
    to me,
"Let us go to the house of the
    Lord!"   122:1

But I through the abundance of thy
    steadfast love
  will enter thy house,
I will worship toward thy holy
    temple   5:7

I *will walk with integrity of heart*
  within my house;
I will not set before my eyes
  anything that is base. 101:2,3

Let the words of my mouth and the
  meditation of my heart
be acceptable in thy sight,
  O Lord, my rock and my
  redeemer. 19:14

PRAISE
THE LORD

Praise the Lord!
Praise, O servants
of the Lord,
praise the name
of the Lord!
Blessed be the name
of the Lord
from this time forth
and for evermore! 113,1-2

F*rom the rising of the sun to its setting*
the name of the Lord is to be praised!
The Lord is high above all nations,
and his glory above the heavens!   113:3-4